ANOLE INVASION

BY MARTA MAGELLAN

ILLUSTRATED BY MAURO MAGELLAN

Eifrig Publishing LLC
Berlin Lemont

In Loving Memory of Sammy Joseph Schnall
2016-2017
M.M.

At Eifrig Publishing, our motto is our mission —
"Good for our kids, good for our Earth, and good for our communities."
We are passionate about helping kids develop into caring, creative, thoughtful individuals who possess positive self-images, celebrate differences, and practice inclusion. Our books promote social and environmental consciousness and empower children as they grow in their communities.
www.eifrigpublishing.com

© 2018 Marta Magellan
Printed in the United States of America

All rights reserved. This publication is protected by Copyright, and permission should be obtained from the publisher prior to any prohibited reproduction, storage in a retrieval system, or transmission in any form or by any means, electronic, mechanical, photocopying, recording, or likewise.

Published by Eifrig Publishing,
PO Box 66, Lemont, PA 16851, USA
Knobelsdorffstr. 44, 14059 Berlin, Germany.

For information regarding permission, write to:
Rights and Permissions Department,
Eifrig Publishing,
PO Box 66, Lemont, PA 16851, USA.
permissions@eifrigpublishing.com, +1-888-340-6543

Library of Congress Cataloging-in-Publication Data
Magellan, Marta
Anole Invasion/
by Marta Magellan, illustrated by Mauro Magellan
p. cm.

Paperback: ISBN 978-1-63233-186-1
Hardcover: ISBN 978-1-63233-187-8
eBook: ISBN 978-1-63233-188-5

[1. Nature – Juvenile Nonfiction. 2. Animals – Anoles, Lizards, Pollinators – Juvenile Nonfiction
I. Magellan, Mauro, ill. II. Title

22 21 20 19 2018
5 4 3 2 1

Printed on recycled PCW acid-free paper. ∞

Science Editor: Kirsten Hines, MS, Biology

Thank you to: Anne Crawford, James Gersing, Kirsten Hines, Silvia Lopez, Rachel Magellan, Ruth Vander Zee, and all the members of the Coral Gables SCBWI picture book writing group. Special thanks to Penny Eifrig and Cathy Snyder whose encouraging support has made this book possible.

A green anole watches a cricket crawl on a branch. The cricket doesn't know it's in danger.

Wild lizards don't have names, but let's call this **green anole** Carolina because it is sometimes known by its common name, Carolina anole.

She stays so still that the cricket doesn't know she's there. Without a sound, she attacks.

The cricket is a goner. Green anoles like Carolina love crickets and beetles and moths. Yuck, they even love cockroaches! But that's good because they help the plants by eating some of the bad bugs in the gardens and forests. They even act as unintentional pollinators by sipping **nectar** (sweet liquid) from flower to flower. **Pollination** is what allows plants to make seeds.

Green anoles are good for plants, but it's about to become harder for Carolina and her friends to visit their usual flowers.

Carolina watches as a small brown lizard scurries through the brush in her **territory** (the area where she lives). The **male** (boy) brown anole bobs his head up and down, does a few push-ups, and flashes his orange **dewlap** (throat fan).

It is a warning.

Carolina turns from green to gray to tan, and finally to dark brown. The invading lizard has put her in a very bad mood!

Green anoles change colors when they feel threatened or sick, or too hot. Because of that, some people call green anoles chameleons. But they are not true chameleons. True chameleons can turn many different colors.

So who was this brown lizard that didn't turn colors at all?

The stranger is a **Cuban brown anole**. It is taking Carolina's territory! Over time, Carolina sees more strange lizards like him. Those brown anoles weren't in the United States at first.

It is called an **invasion**. How did that happen?

About a hundred years ago in Cuba, a brown anole hitched a ride on a boat. Let's call her Cubanita.

When Cubanita tried to leave, the ocean stretched out all around. Soon, the boat docked. Cubanita quickly sped off the boat and looked around her new home. Where was she?

The place was warm, humid, and full of palm trees and shrubs. She had landed in Florida. She found some moist leaf litter and laid an egg.

Every week or two during that summer, she laid one or two eggs. Over time, little brown anoles were everywhere. Then a bigger, meaner anole invaded Florida.

© istock/Patrick Gijsbers

In the 1950's, the big-headed Knight Anole hitched a ride to Florida, too. It also came from Cuba. It became more of a threat because it eats the smaller anoles!

And that's not all. It eats frogs and baby birds, too. And that wasn't the last of the invasions.

Around 1975 a new enemy invaded, this time from Puerto Rico. The crested anole fought harder and ran faster than both the green and brown anoles.

After the crested anoles invaded, brown anoles moved to middle levels of the plants and trees. Two other invaders, the giant anole from Jamaica and the bark anole from Haiti, have also made their way into Florida.

There isn't enough food in the lower plants for all of them to share. Carolina and her relatives had to find another way to stay alive.

Invaders are not good for native green anoles like Carolina. The different **species** (types) of lizards compete for the same food. Worse, the non-native anoles eat the eggs of the green anole. The invaders eat more of the food. So the green anoles have to climb higher up in the plants, and even higher in the trees.

This is called **displacement.** And that's trouble.

Cuban brown anoles have now spread out to other parts of the southern United States. Crested anoles and Knight anoles have wandered north to Central Florida. They are roaming even farther up, displacing more green anoles.

When invasive species have been living in a place long enough, scientists say they are **established**. To stay alive, green anoles have to make changes.

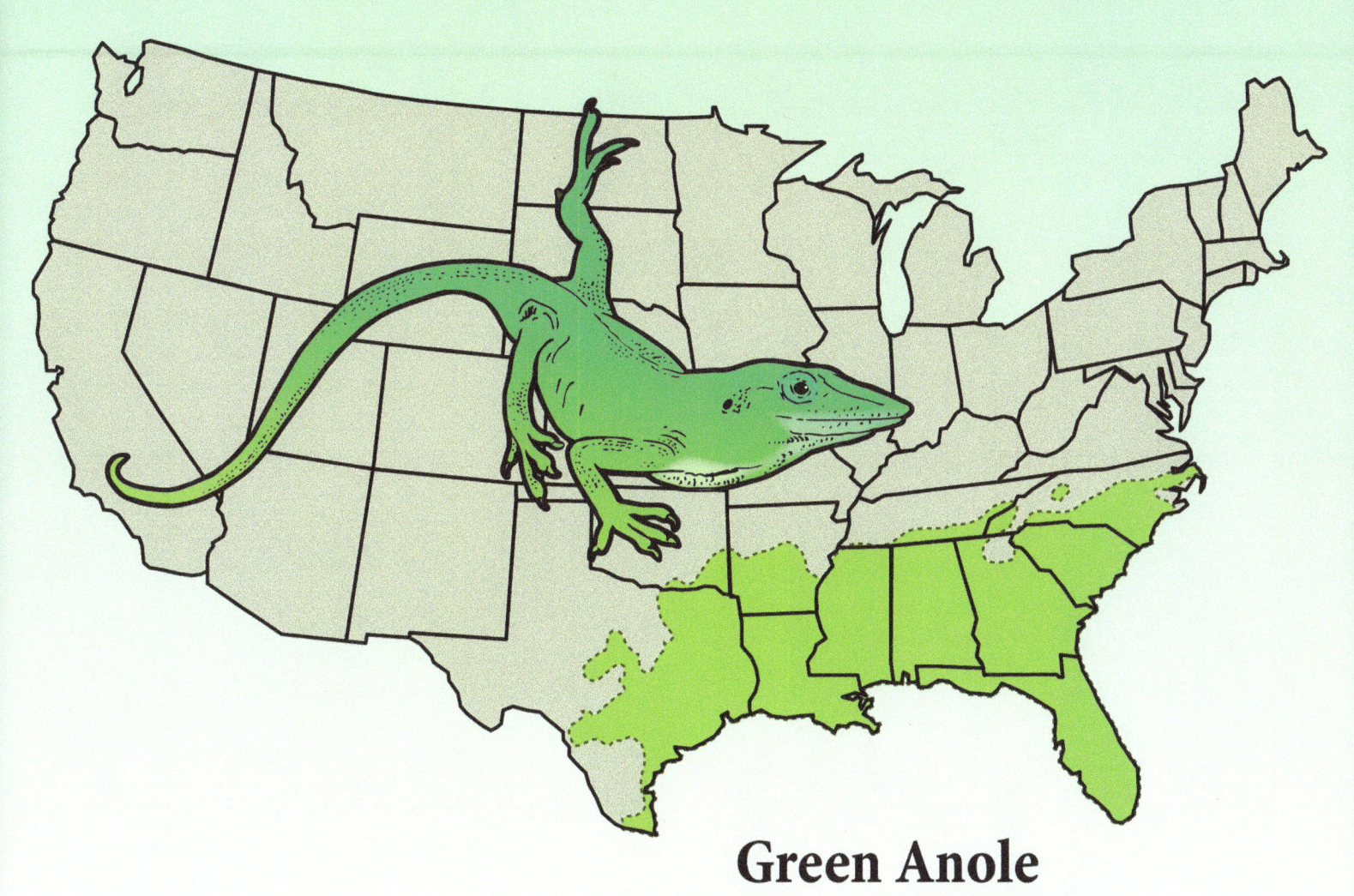

Green Anole
Anolis carolinensis

The good news is, green anoles are not **extinct**. Far from it! So far, they aren't **endangered**, either. They are alive and well in most of the southeastern United States.

When they climb higher up in trees because the invasive species are in their territory, it is called **adapting**.

Humans need to be careful not to let invasive species of any kind overrun native territories like those of the green anole. We need green anoles in our gardens and forests to help plants grow. As long as they keep adapting, they will stay off the endangered list and help our flowers and plants thrive.

GLOSSARY

Adaptation: The changes over time in behavior of structure of an organism (living thing) to become more suited to its surroundings.

Anole: A small lizard that lives in bushes and climbs trees.

Dewlap: A usually bright colored flap of skin on the throat that lizards display on purpose to communicate. It flares out like a fan when the male lizard feels threatened or wants to attract a mate.

Displacement: When two competing species want to live in the same place, the weaker animal will be forced to move to new territory because there will not be enough places to live or food to share.

Endangered: A plant or animal species in danger of becoming extinct.

Extinct: When the last member of a species has died and that animal no longer exists.

Female: The girl sex of an animal, which produces eggs.

Invasive/Invasion: When non-native species have been brought to a location by humans and become so successful that they displace the native species.

Male: The boy sex on an animal that fertilizes the female's eggs and turns them into babies.

Native: In biology, it means animals that normally have lived in a particular location for hundreds of years or more and were not brought in by humans.

Pollination: When pollen from plants is moved from the male part of the plant to the female part to form seeds.

Species: A group of closely related animals that are physically similar and are usually capable of reproducing (having babies).

Territory: An area where a single animal, or group of the same species lives and defends against invaders.

SOME INTERESTING FACTS

Crested Anole: *Anolis cristatellus cristatellus*
A lizard native to Puerto Rico. The crested anole has become invasive in South Florida. It feeds on insects, blossoms, and fruit. It has displaced the Cuban brown anole, which first displaced the green anole.

Chameleon: Chamaeleonidae
A colorful lizard native to Africa and Asia, these striking lizards are known for their ability to change color. There are many different species of chameleons, and they come in a variety of brilliant colors. They have a long, sticky tongue; and their eyes can be moved independently of each other.

Cuban Anole: *Anolis sagrei sagrei*
A small brown lizard native to Cuba that has become an invasive species in Florida and a few other southeastern states.

Green Anole: *Anolis carolinensis*

A small green lizard native to the southeastern United States. Green anoles are the only anoles native to the U.S. They change colors from green to brown for reasons such as health, mood, temperature, but not necessarily to blend into their surroundings.

Knight Anole: *Anolis equestris equestris*

A medium-sized lizard originally from Cuba that has become an invasive species in several Florida counties. It is known to prey upon smaller anoles, frogs, and baby birds.

ABOUT THE AUTHOR AND ILLUSTRATOR

Marta Magellan and Mauro Magellan are a brother and sister team that have collaborated on this book. Marta Magellan is a children's book writer, with special interest in nature topics. She is retired from Miami Dade College where she taught Composistion, Creative Writing, and Survey of Children's Literature as a full professor. She has written travel articles, essays, and children's books for the educational market. More information can be found on her website at: www.martamagellan.com

Mauro Magellan is an illustrator, graphic artist, and musician who has written and illustrated children's books as well as nonfiction for adults through Pelican Press, Scholastic, Long Street Press, and others. He is also a professional graphic designer who creates artwork and branding for billboards, brochures, posters, and print media in general. Interested in all the arts, he is a songwriter and drummer, currently playing with the popular Nashville-based band, *Dan Baird and Homade Sin* and traveling throughout Europe with *The Jimmys,* an award-winning nine-piece horn band. Check out his website: www.magellanartdesign.com

ABOUT THE SCIENCE EDITOR

Kirsten Hines, M.Sc. in biology, is an environmental educator, writer, and photographer, focused on conservation. Raised in the Philippines but based in Miami since 1998, she has published 30 journal articles and technical reports on flora and fauna, mostly from South Florida and the Caribbean. She has also co-authored three books about South Florida: *Attracting Birds to South Florida Gardens*, *Key Biscayne*, and *Biscayne National Park*. www.kirstennaturetravel.com

OTHER BOOKS BY MARTA MAGELLAN AND MAURO MAGELLAN WITH EIFRIG PUBLISHING

The Nutty Little Vulture
by Marta Magellan
Illustrated by Mauro Magellan
2018, Eifrig Publishing
This picture book is about a little vulture, who unlike others like him, wants to eat only palm nuts. It is based on true behavior of real vultures in Africa, but fictionalized and illustrated for the very young. This is a scrumptious book introducing the importance of vultures to children.

Felicia and the Rat (book and music)
Written, Illustrated and Composed by Mauro Magellan
2018, Eifrig Publishing
Louie lives high up on a rooftop. He likes to play the drums and one day dreams of playing along with the professional musician cats. There is only one problem. Louie, well…he's a rat. What cat would play with a rat? Includes 11 original soundtracks for instant listening.

Watercolor Leaf Assets by Octopus Artis via designcuts.com

INDEX

(numbers in bold refer to photographs or illustrations)

adaptation, adapting, 24, 25
bark anole, 18
brown anole, Cuban brown anole, 8, **9**, 12, **13**, 14, 18, 22
Carolina anole, green anole, 5, 6, **7**, 18, **20**, 21, 22, **23**, 24, 25
chameleon, **10**, 11
color change, 11
competetion, compete, 21, 22
crested anole, 18, **19**
Cuba, 14, 17
dewlap, 8, **9**
displacement, 21, 22
eggs, 14, 15, 21
endangered, 25
established, 22
extinct, 25
Florida, 14, 17
flowers, plants, 6, 7, 14, 18, 21, 25
food, **4**, 5, 6, **7**, 17, 18, 21
giant anole, 18
green anole, Carolina anole, 5, 6, **7**, 18, **20**, 21, 22, **23**, 24, 25
invasion, invaders, 12, 17, 18, 21, 22, 24
knight anole, **16**, 17, 22
male, 8
nectar, 6
pollination, pollinators, 6, 7
Puerto Rico, 18
species, 21, 22, 24
territory, 8, 12, 18, 21, **23**, 24, 25

www.ingramcontent.com/pod-product-compliance
Lightning Source LLC
Chambersburg PA
CBHW040010080526
44586CB00028B/2959